Jeanne Willis

Illustrated by Robert Eberz

Rigby
A Harcourt Achieve Imprint

www.Rigby.com
1-800-531-5015

One autumn morning, Paula woke at dawn to hear a strange sound. It sounded like a cat meowing, but not quite. Her sister Laura came into her room.

"Do you hear a funny noise?" Laura asked.

"Yes, it's coming from outside," said Paula.

They quietly crept down the hall to the stairs. Their parents were sound asleep. Paula opened the front door.

Paula gasped. There was a small, metal cat sitting on the porch. It had wire whiskers and glowing eyes.

"It's a robot-cat!" Paula said.

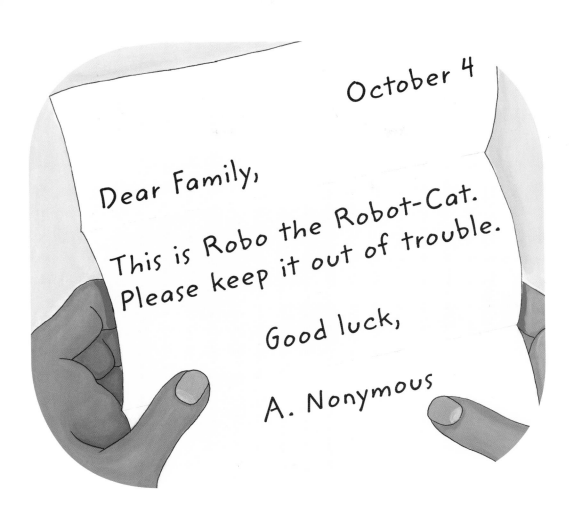

October 4

Dear Family,

This is Robo the Robot-Cat.
Please keep it out of trouble.

Good luck,

A. Nonymous

A letter was tied to its neck.
Paula read it out loud.

"I wonder why someone left it on our porch. And how could it possibly get into trouble?"

Robo meowed. "Maybe it's lonely," said Laura.

"Oh, Laura," laughed Paula. "It's a robot, not a cat! Machines can't get lonely."

"We have to give it a home," said Laura. Laura and Paula weren't allowed to have a cat. But a *robot*-cat couldn't be too much trouble, could it?

Laura carried Robo into the kitchen. Its metal parts squeaked.

"Shh," said Paula. "The noise will wake Mom and Dad."

"A drink of milk will fix it," Laura said.

"Oh, Laura, you can't do that. It's a robot, not a cat!" said Paula. "Milk will clog its gears."

Paula put some oil onto Robo's moving parts. The squeaking stopped.

"Now it's oily," said Laura.
"Robo needs a bath."

"Oh, Laura, you can't do that.
It's a robot, not a cat!" said
Paula. "Water will make it rust."

Paula got some metal polish
and a cloth instead. She polished
Robo until it was shiny.

Robo's metal jaw opened and its eyes blinked.

Laura picked up the robot-cat and put it in her doll's bed. "Robo yawned. I'll put it to bed," said Laura.

"Oh, Laura, you can't do that. It's a robot, not a cat!" said Paula. "Turn it off."

Paula pressed the power button on its chest. Robo's eyes went dark.

"But I'd rather play," said Laura. She threw a ball. "Go get it, Robo!" she said.

"Oh, Laura, you can't do that. It's a robot, not a cat!" said Paula. "First turn it back on."

Laura tried to press the power button, but she didn't know which one it was. She pressed all the buttons at once.

Suddenly, Robo sparked.

"MEOW!" Robo shot into the kitchen. It skidded past the sink and smashed some plates.

"Oh, no! It's lost a spring!" cried Paula.

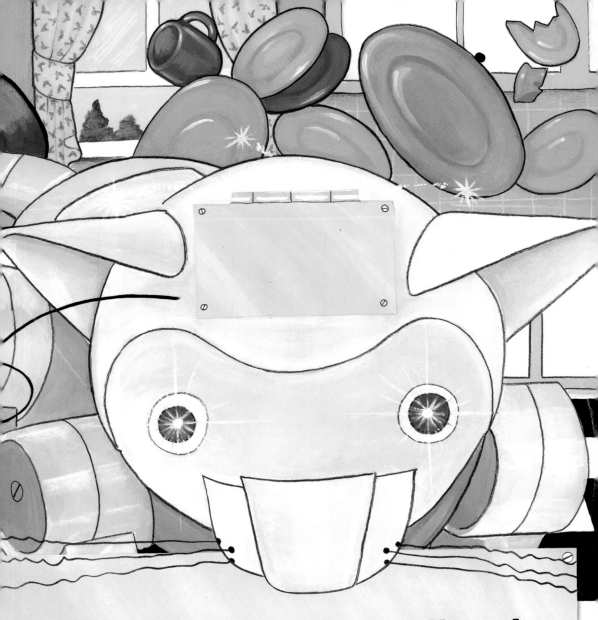

It crashed into the wall and knocked off all the pans. Laura and Paula tried to catch Robo, but it rolled too fast.

"MEOW!" Robo rolled into the hall. It raced up the wall and scratched the wallpaper.

Robo's wheels knocked all the pictures onto the floor.

"Oh, no! It's lost a gear!" cried Laura. Robo headed for the living room. Paula and Laura tried to keep up.

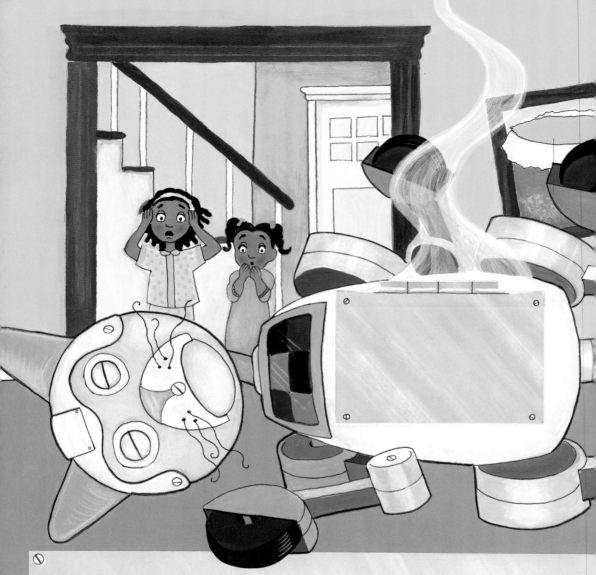

"MEOW!" Robo pulled down the curtains.

It landed on the bookcase. Crash! The bookcase fell and smashed a lamp.

"Oh, no! It's lost a screw!"
cried Paula. "Catch it, Laura!"
Suddenly, Robo stopped. It fell
onto its side and was still. Its
motor had come loose.

"The noise probably woke Mom and Dad. Quick, help me fix Robo before they come downstairs," said Paula.

They opened Robo's panels and put its parts back inside.

Paula snapped the motor in place. Robo's eyes lit up.

Just then, their parents came down the stairs and stopped.

"What in the world happened?" asked their mother.

"Can we keep it?" said Laura, petting Robo. "It's only a robot."

"It'll be no trouble at all!" said Paula.